Fifties Homestyle

Fifties Homestyle

POPULAR ORNAMENT OF THE USA

Mark Burns &
Louis DiBonis
PHOTOGRAPHS BY
Norinne Betjemann

Foreword by PETER DORMER

PERENNIAL LIBRARY

HARPER & ROW, PUBLISHERS, New York
Cambridge, Philadelphia, San Francisco, Washington
London, Mexico City, São Paulo, Singapore, Sydney

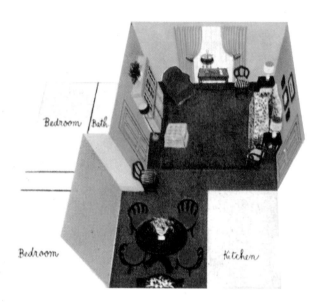

Bedroom / Bath

Bedroom

Kitchen

First PERENNIAL LIBRARY Edition published 1988.

ISBN 0–06–097176–2 (pbk.)

88 89 90 91 RRD 10 9 8 7 6 5 4 3 2 1

Contents

Foreword

The row house in Philadelphia gives nothing away from the outside. But when you are invited through the entrance for the first time, you are at once visually winded: the lobby is adorned with plastic Christs and Virgin Mary table lamps; then, as you enter the first floor living area, a cornucopia of 1950s consumerism spills out. You left outside a wide, uncomforting street of utilitarian buildings and used car lots—no nonsense America. Inside you are suddenly eyeballing domestic America at play. It is warm, fascinating, dazzling, and unsettling all at the same time.

In this house, Mark Burns and Louis DiBonis have assembled a vast array of things that ordinary middle-majority Americans bought for their homes during the 1950s. What you are looking at is not an aberration but an important part of the core of America's modern culture. This—stuff—was the norm, therefore it cannot be eccentric. This is not minority taste, but majority choice encouraged, naturally, by that great engine for production and wealth that America has so artfully shaped for the world—mass advertising.

Burns is an artist, he is a wiry, perceptive, and sharply intelligent man. He finds his stuff fascinating, good fun, sometimes sad. He and his partner Louis DiBonis, who in recent years has become as great a supplicant to the collection as Burns himself, have built a collection which demonstrates many positive things about American culture of the time: it was inventive, opportunistic, and democratic.

What we are looking at is America at the height of its mass manufacturing prowess, with a million companies small and large seizing on new materials and processes to satisfy a demand for new things across a wide range of prices.

Nearly everyone, except the very poor, could find crockery, cutlery, ornaments, kitchen and bathroom accessories—you named it, you could have it—at a price you could afford. Democratic America.

Is it kitsch? If kitsch is, as some people think, the result of stealing the surface effects of mature cultures, then this work, with its concatenation of ethnic, religious, and Hollywood images, is kitsch. But all cultures take ideas from others and it is clear that what Mark and Louis have accumulated is the fantastic outpouring of a culture that is itself mature. It had the technology, the ideals, and a clear self-identity which it fed through its manufacturings. America in the 1950s was unique; it invented a cheap consumer society which, with its fantastic advertising industry, created a model of capitalist choice and excess which many other countries, most of them much older than America, raided in their turn.

And it is the glorious, fat, creamy American originals—now enthusiastically collected again—that Mark and Lou invite you to enjoy.

PETER DORMER
Design Analysis International Ltd

A Real American Mix

Do you think that time travel is possible? We do. Once inside our house, the present ceases to exist, and you find yourself falling into the Time of Great Promise, the American Fifties. Behind the mild-mannered façade of our Philadelphia row house (and its permanently covered front windows) the past rages from room to room, living up to its reputation, demanding attention, irritating, cajoling, shouting for your time, love, and mental health. The sheer number of artefacts we have amassed speaks visually of all that was New! Improved! and—let's not forget—Atomic! The portrait of a decade emerges: the most hopeful and neurotic of times for the great middle majority. Our recollection of that decade may be distorted by the passing years, even though we grew up in the thick of it, but we have the tangible evidence that our combined memories have not deceived us entirely.

Blue collar upbringing provided a similar background for both of us. Louis was raised in the working-class district of urban Philadelphia and Mark grew up in the heartland of Ohio. Louis's father was a driver for the sanitation department; Mark's father built refrigerators and washing machines. Our mothers worked in menial jobs and kept house for their husbands.

We lived in extremely middle-majority neighborhoods: our houses were cracker box or row houses in areas characterized by complete anonymity. The only real difference between Louis's urban environment and Mark's rural one lay in transport: in the country, you needed an automobile; in the city, you could make do with public transport.

It seems to us, although we are not social historians, that in that time everything was geared to the family unit. In the wider world, it felt as if the war(s) had passed away—at least after Korea. The Bomb was a daily—but somehow remote— companion, and everything was possible.

Many families had a brand-new house, a car, a TV, and a washer (the dryer would take years to show up.) That was typical. But once they had the necessities, the people hankered after more. The rise of the middle-majority decorative object was swift in response to that longing. And because everyone had some money to spend on home decoration, the great emporiums of Sears, Penneys and Woolworths offered bountiful selections at modest prices. The concept of House Beautiful on a shoestring was born.

Designers were quick to see the void for New Objects, and rushed to fill it by using the materials and technology that Helped Us Win The War in a less destructive but no less aggressive direction. Observe, please, the radical changes in something as simple as color schemes.

After the long, dull Forties, why hang on to tired browns, plums and greys? Why not jazz up everything with chartreuse or flamingo pink? New color meant New attitude, and so we had a blinding array of objects which could not sit quietly, from fabric coverings to clothing to the dishes we ate from. Everybody knew that in the Future (which was Now), this was just how it ought to be. Color was only the beginning—the tip of the melting iceberg. If the buying public was being seduced (and they were a cheap date) by the attraction of new hues, why put up with Granny's furniture? Why not get some new? The Future had better things to offer—a plethora of boomerangs, amoebas, kidney shapes, triangles, sticks, stars, cocktail cherry legs, obtuse angles. And who cared if it was uncomfortable? It was the Future! We could adapt! It was all so easy to care for, too. Wash 'n' Wear! Drip Dry! Sanforized! Quickly we were confronted with a bewildering amount of alien furniture, shapes and colors. They were easily had—no down payment—and just the thing for keeping up with the neighbors.

Once the process of filling up a living space had begun in the Fifties, the problem became—not where to choose from—but what to choose. There was a mind-boggling selection of consumer goods.

Americans have always prided themselves on being able to have it all, and industry was quick to reinforce this particular idea. Mass-manufacturing made all things available in all price ranges to allow even the poorest family to array its home in dimestore splendor. No matter that the glamor was composed of plaster and cheap plastic, it looked good. And when the thing lost its luster, or was broken (whichever came first), it could be tossed away and replaced with something equally beautiful and inexpensive.

Home decoration suddenly became a major complication for the newly elevated Modern Housewife. For instance, after the furniture was placed and the coverings determined, what *was* one to do with the TV? The screen was fine, but the box it sat in became a dreaded Dead Spot in the otherwise lovely living room. Recommended lighting for proper viewing called for low-wattage illumination and, suddenly, an industry was born. A primal icon was invented, and it filled the dead spot: The TV lamp.

The TV lamp decorated a blighted space, it did not hurt your eyes, and it came in a vast variety of sizes and types.

Madam! we Challenge you

TO EXPRESS A COLOR PREFERENCE IN
CARPETING WHICH WE CAN'T MEET!

Indeed, all lighting fixtures suddenly became major focal points in the overall decor of the Fifties household. Imagery was rampant, albeit of a singularly strange type. Our interest in cultures exotic and unusual exploded in lamp-base design. Thus we saw Russian ballerinas vaulting Japanese bonsai trees that held Bauhaus shapes for shades—in fact, one could compose an almost endless list of the bizarre hybrid mixes that were made, and sold.

Who cared if it didn't all fit together? It looked good, and looking good was all that mattered. The use of non-U.S. cultures could be seen in all decorative objects, not merely lamps. We appropriated cultural particulars and turned them into stereotypes. There was no longer a place in the marketplace for overt racism of the kind that gave birth to the black-face "mammy" object. Racism resurfaced, instead, in non-specific "Oriental" figures who always wore coolie hats and pajamas, or with Mexicans who seem always to be enjoying a fiesta and carry maracas and pottery, or with the Dutch, forever trapped into tending tulips and clumping about in clogs.

Our collective consciousness allowed us to share our homes and hearths with these outsiders because they were invariably presented as safe, smiling and sanitized. They brought a degree of the exotic into our ordinary lives, and the native strangeness fueled our sharpening sense for the absurd.

Sex was then (as now) most certainly on everyone's mind. The Fifties saw the loosening of public morals and an easing of a prudishness that had been almost nineteenth century in its effort to keep passion in check.

Even so the goal of women was assumed to be marriage. An advertisement for a Mercury automobile tells it all: "She's married—She's happy—She drives a Mercury." And why especially a Mercury? It has a glove compartment big enough for his and her stuff. What's more—the advertisement goes on to ask— "And ladies, Do you hide the bill from the gas station till your husband's in a good humor?" The answer: "Not if you own a Mercury ... your gas bills are low."

Being children at this time meant conforming to the same stereotyping of pairing. Girls were really housewives in training, but boys were luckier in having semi-fictions like cowboys to model themselves on. The girls had their toy tin cookers to play with, the boys had cowboy suits, guns and Buckin' Broncko wallpaper. The ideal was man and wife, son and daughter, happy pairings servicing one another in the roles set down by the church and the advertising industry. Children were processed by their non-thinking parents and also by outside influences such as the guru of the confused Atomic family—Dr. Spock. But even Spock's influence paled compared to

She's married—She's happy— She drives a **MERCURY**

MERCURY DIVISION OF FORD MOTOR COMPANY

that of the television, which became the babysitter of the decade.

American children, hypnotized by the magic box, came to worship at the electronic altar, where the infant entertainment industry decreed that Saturday mornings would be the time to pay proper respect. Thus, children's programing was born, producing one of the first really popular children's shows, Howdy Doody. Howdy was a wooden marionette of a rather androgynous nature (although it wore a cowboy outfit), and was partnered on the screen by a human called Buffalo Bob. The immense success of this program was followed quickly by other series using/imitating the adult-child "sidekick" format. This "child-as-minature-adult" idea reinforced the viewer's duties and responsibilities, as well as stressing the all-important family unit.

What kid could resist (or forget?) the adventures of Superman and Jimmy Olsen, Sky King and his niece Penny, Annie Oakley and Tagg, or even Wonder Dog Rin Tin Tin and his aide-de-camp Rusty? There were heroes and heroines enough for all, both boys and girls! For those few hours once a week, we were invincible. And to remind us the rest of the week, we carried lunch boxes to school emblazoned with those self-same heroes. In our collection, we have dozens of these boxes, which reflect a TV pantheon, as well as the more popular childhood fantasies, again just like the ones we saw on TV.

The glamor of TV touched everyone. And, since everything was advertising and consumer led, the adults were soon enjoying the delights of TV Christianity (one of the early major clerics of the tube was Bishop Sheen). But more secular delights prospered, especially the drag acts of the variety performer Milton Berle. And although radio drama was still important in the early Fifties—romantic serials such as "The Shadows" were popular—once radio gave way to TV, the soap opera was begotten. As everyone knows, these programs were vehicles for the washing powder ads aimed directly at the housewife.

The Fifties were ambivalent about sexual licence. As I said earlier, people were obsessed by the subject; new diversions such as the 29 cent 45 r.p.m. discs and Elvis Presley and rock 'n' roll were seen by the young as delightful, but by some of the Elders as taboo. TV cameras, for example, were not at first permitted to show Elvis from anything other than the waist up—those gyrations of his were too much to bring into the parlor.

Reading did not disappear, despite the predictions of school teachers. Children devoured adventure books—oriented by sex, of course. The boys read "The Hardy Boys" and the girls identified with a heroine called Nancy Drew—she was always getting into scrapes. Housewives read magazines and wrote letters to them; and some of them certainly felt that the American dream was true.

This letter from *True Story* (a monthly magazine) was not untypical:

I've been reading True Story *ever since I learned English, and I feel that it has helped me to become an American, truly. And every time I finish a story, I realize again that the American man is the finest in the world. In Hungary, where I come from, a woman is like a slave at home. Whatever a husband says is what is done. Cooking and housework is a woman's job and a man would not think of helping his wife ever. Even heavy farm work she does alone if he is tired. I'm happy and proud that I came to this country and married an American boy, where work is fifty-fifty in the family. I hope to raise my two children in the good free American way of living. That when they grow up and marry, they know how to share life with another. Like we said at the altar—for better or worse, in health or in illness.*

From Mrs S.H., a two-year American.

If the Fifties were a golden age for America, and advertising and TV told us all that this America was IT!, the country did not feel like paradise to everyone. A lot of the work which earned the material wealth was repetitious. People did work hard. And our complacency was wafer thin. Apparently (although we were too young to realize it at the time) our national self-confidence was temporarily knocked when the Soviets put up a Sputnik in 1957. Still, it made a great tee-shirt image.

Amid the color there was drabness—that's why so many bought so much to disguise it. Nevertheless, America is presented, and used to present itself, as a creamy sort of place—full of things. I've noted that whenever our most acerbic social commentator, Tom Wolfe, wants to give the country's texture he draws up great lists of American goodies. Take this one, from a scene he wrote in "Mau Mauing the Flak Catchers": "hot dogs, tacos, Whammies, Frostees, Fudgiscles, french fries, Eskimo Pies, Awful-Awfuls, Sugar-Daddies, Sugar-Mommies, Sugar-Babies, Chocolate-covered frozen bananas, malted milks, Yoo-Hoos, berry pies, bubble gums, cotton candy, Space food sticks, Frescas, Baskins-Robbins, Boysenberry-cheesecake, ice cream cones, Milky Ways, M & Ms, Tootsie Pops, Slurpees, Drumsticks, jelly doughnuts, taffy apples, buttered Karamel Korn, root-beer floats, Hi-C punches, large Cokes, 7-Ups, Three-Musketeers bars, frozen Kool-Aids."

Ours is an inventive country. We are good at satisfying the demands of people on low income for quasi-luxury consumerables—whether for mass-manufactured "toy" food and candy like that on Tom Wolfe's list, or for the plastic baroque that you will find in our collection.

And, of course, what you see in this book is a collection. The larger-format shots are of rooms in *our* house, they are not shots of a typical piece of Levitt Town. No one, other than ourselves, has thirty TV lamps in one room, for example. Living in this environment is not an attempt at living in the past, but it is like a 3D scrapbook of many people (their tastes and hopes, even their neuroses) and places. It is a living montage of the styles and obsessions that molded our formative years, but we do not wallow in it—we are fascinated by it, marveling at the ingenuity, and enjoying the overwhelming impact of it all when one sees it *en masse*.

We have been collecting this stuff for many years now. We are not in love with bad taste; nor do we feel some kind of inverse snobbery at being surrounded by "kitsch." As Peter Dormer observes in his foreword, these pieces are not "kitsch," they are the thing itself—the heart of American Culture. Quite a number of the artefacts—especially for daily kitchen use—are well designed. They make attractive use of modern techniques, such as the anodizing of metals, and of new materials: plastics technology developed rapidly in the 1950s. Moreover, much of the graphic work—printed textiles such as tee-shirts and tablecloths, posters, or printed plastic laminates—has a clarity, directness and intelligence that has since been recognized by avant-garde designers in Europe who have then re-exported it to the States under the guise of post-modernism.

Shame on our style gurus, they never recognized it.

Good product design, seen here in a food mixer and a coffee pot, was as much a feature of the Fifties as non-functional design.

Fabric prints such as these from the mid-1950s were certainly not "high culture." With high culture, surfaces had to be plain. The middle majority would have none of *that* nonsense; it liked *everything* covered.

The organization and structure of the pattern making are good and inventive. The patterns also fall into salesmen's categories—we have lyrical modern (*above*), modern traditional (*right*), and visual rock 'n' roll (*opposite*). But the underlying style and quality behind each different pattern remain the same: simple, graphic, loud—they unload themselves on you in one go. What is clear, as we look back, is the sharpness of the statement, "we are NEW."

The graphic style was rooted in magazine advertising and illustration, although many of the motifs are adapted from the modern art of the period—the dance of the kidneys above and the edgy, jumping bacteria opposite read like the commercial artist's view of the modern art of the period.

There was a severe case of follow the Leda throughout the Fifties. Swans, with their serpentine necks and sumptuous feathers, made popular ornament. A swan motif is graphically malleable: you can bunch it up or elongate it; and, of course, swans make good pairs. In this detail (*left*), we have made a feature of these plaster plaques and have even created a touch of heraldry.

Our house is decorated to complement the collection, while remaining true to the period in color and style. We have, however, made our decor a little theatrical—which is fair, since this is a knowing collection, not a representation of what the ordinary home looked like.

Our living and lounge areas are hung with movie posters from the Fifties: the movie fantasies still fed our imaginations as potently as the TV in those days.

The flamingo is a natural for exotic ornament, as are such creatures as panthers, leopards, cheetahs and things that go growl in the night. The degree of accuracy is minimal. These plaster and cast ceramic beasts are generalized ornaments and it is doubtful whether anyone ever linked them with nature, especially since the emphasis was on what was manmade. Their pedigree is the cartoon.

Chinamen and Mexicans were represented as childlike, innocent, fun loving—and lazy. White folk were the serious adults, brown and yellow people were engaging, the Korean War notwithstanding. These objects were born out of ignorance, reinforced by TV and the developing tourist trade and its propaganda. Of course, the relative simplicity of the component forms is a result of a manufacturing process using low-grade technology.

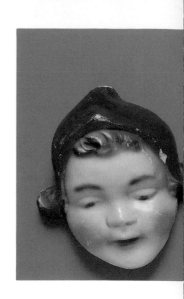

Women were widely seen as domestic servants, and the male/female stereotypes began at an early age—little boys and big boys knew that Mom would clean up after them. The NEW detergent helped.

Children became identified in the Fifties as a vast consumer group, and endless products were devised and adapted especially for them—the kids were a powerful highway to Dad's pocketbook.

Plastic and plaster religious artefacts decorated with seashells found contented purchasers in a society that put Christianity onto the television screen and swiftly allied it to big business.

This Champion spark plug is a promotional gift, a working radio with the on/off knob and tuner at the top. The Mickey Mouse face is in fact a camera, and is a good example of the way America pioneered the art of the "spin off" product. This is a field characterized by great ingenuity and lateral thinking. However, the Soviet Union was into "spin offs" of its own, notably the Sputnik launched in 1957. The apparent technological lead by the Russians may have scared the Pentagon, but an American businessman swiftly saw an opening and celebrated the event with a quick tee shirt. Leisure was another industry the USA pioneered as a growth, moneymaking area—tenpin bowling became as "All American" as Cola.

FAIRLANES BOWLING

Sputniks

Chapman

COTTMAN LANES PRO SHOP

The Soft Hiss of
Vinyl under a
Californian Shade

The living room of the American 1950s was not for living in. Today, our own "living" room merely exaggerates what was central to the real living room of millions of Americans—formality and a museum-like aspect. No one actually lived in these spaces. Traditionally, the parlor—predecessor of the living room—was a dead area. Then it evolved into something more theatrical; it became the family's showing-off and acting-up space: a room enlivened when "company" came, and the air was invaded by cries of admiration as your friends and relatives discovered your most beautiful possessions set out in those formal arrangements, designed by you to show everything up to its best advantage.

Sundays and the living room and "company manners" went together when we were children in the Fifties. In the Fifties, Benjamin Spock notwithstanding, the middle-majority child was to be seen and not heard too much. The grown-ups would sit and chat, we would sit and sit—and sit. There would be oases. Drinking milk from a jelly glass was one. For once the last sip of milk from the glass was taken, at the bottom a 3D image of a Howdy Doody show personality would "appear." As the milk drained away, the interested child would want to see who was being revealed. Adult conversation would be rent by: "I got Buffalo Bill." After this highlight, the Sunday would go dead. One hoped for a quick release to home and the TV.

But why continue in the past tense? Now, as then, all activity necessarily centers around the coffee table, that ingenious American invention which becomes the nucleus of the room's activity. Your lovely furniture should encompass, in close proximity, the invaluable table for entertaining and social activity. Upon this altar of gracious living, you might find ashtrays, cigarette boxes and coasters on the upper glass level: the aim is effortless entertaining.

The coffee table thus fixes the nucleus from which radiate the major circles defined by such totem items as the sofa and the occasional chairs. We are teased by the surreal description, so redolent of that mixed-up decade, of chairs being "occasional." What are they when they are not being chairs? Nor must we forget the double-decker end tables—for these are the punctuation marks in the room's vocabulary. Ideally, they should flank the behemoth of the sofa and hold the omnipresent ornamental lamps, which usually have a plastic figure for a base and always come in pairs—male and female.

Those lamps tell you a lot about Fifties society and the emphasis on the idea of the happy couple. The living room, where you entertained Company, was the place to reinforce the stereotype that you were a couple (whatever rows you might have in the kitchen). This singular neurotic sensibility about happy pairing becomes evident where figurative ornament is concerned because we see that for every boy there had to be a girl—no matter how sexually ambiguous the boy. Every animal had its mate, and so the concept of pairing was reinforced through ornament. Mrs. Housewife certainly had no problem in choosing happy couples of any ethnic flavor to enhance her choice of theme. Matador and Matador<u>ette</u>, Nubian and Nubian<u>ette</u>: we see that in all presentations and objects everything was touched by and smothered with overtones of the contented and complementary twosome.

Observation will tell you that the truly great living rooms not only work in circular arrangements but on a variety of levels of mass. A really fine living room space works naturally at each level, with the foundation defined by a floral or plain scroll-worked carpet. The ether is lit by a ubiquitous split-level Californian shade under whose green light one will encounter bumpers of plaster fruit, or a flock of plastic parrots, or the ever upwardly mobile plastic prima ballerinas.

Of course, in our living room, as in all our rooms, we have violated the rule of pairs by insisting on multiples of everything possible. Our principle seeks to over-egg the already rich American mix: if two seashell lamps are good, then twenty are better. If two flamingoes set a mood of old Miami, will not a flock conjure up the entire state of Florida? We believe excess equals better living.

To complete the repertoire, there is the china closet which in true Fifties fashion does not contain china but the artefacts and souvenirs you wish to preserve in this museum-to-yourself.

Dedicated as we are to the idea that nothing succeeds like excess, we find that, because we can never make up our minds about fabric patterns, we include all our current favorites—in the appropriate places, naturally. Carpet, drapes, pillows, dust covers, and upholstery provide geometrics and florals in profusion. *Good* taste (which is always ascetic) would declare that these patterns should never be seen *en masse* because they cannot *possibly* work in unison. Yet, in the sheer weight of abundance, they *do*.

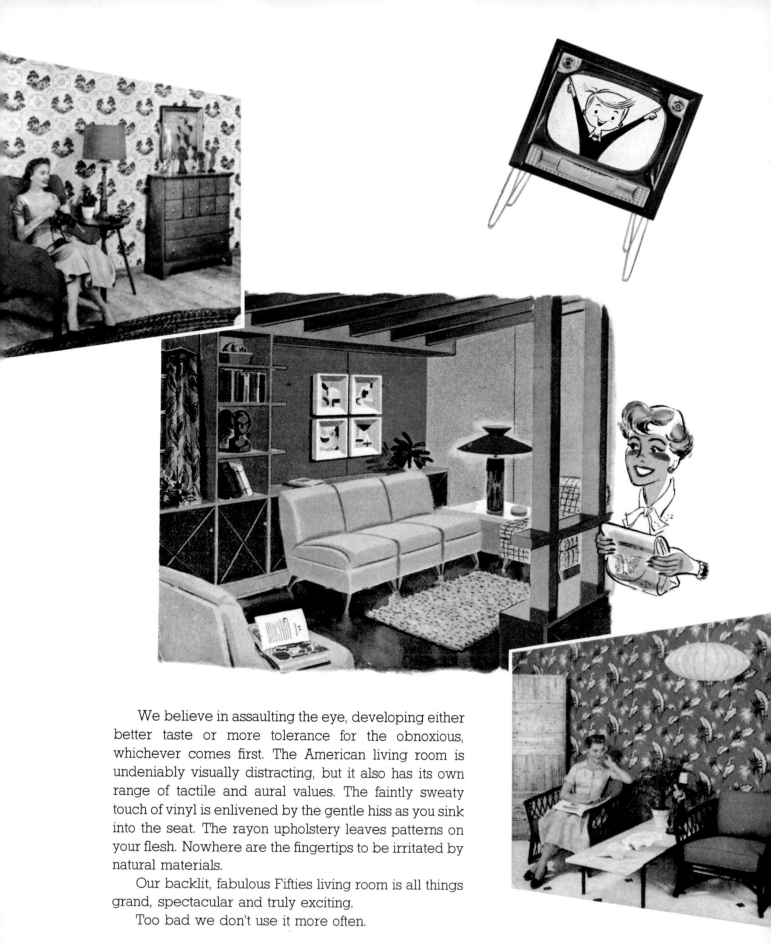

We believe in assaulting the eye, developing either better taste or more tolerance for the obnoxious, whichever comes first. The American living room is undeniably visually distracting, but it also has its own range of tactile and aural values. The faintly sweaty touch of vinyl is enlivened by the gentle hiss as you sink into the seat. The rayon upholstery leaves patterns on your flesh. Nowhere are the fingertips to be irritated by natural materials.

Our backlit, fabulous Fifties living room is all things grand, spectacular and truly exciting.

Too bad we don't use it more often.

Good modern taste (*left*) went for a pared down, angular look—in a sense, it reciprocated the leggy stiletto ideal in modern women. However, real taste preferred robust sumptuousness, with armchairs built like behemoths. These were nearly always covered in an all-over pattern that was wrinkled like the grey matter of a whale. One of the characteristics of American taste is, or was, a preference for perceived weight and gravitas, as well as elaboration. Without "weight" and "elaboration" the consumer felt he or she was not getting value for money.

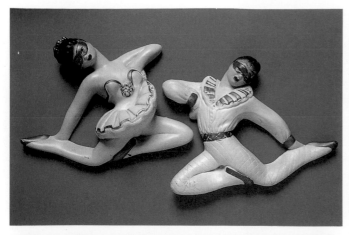

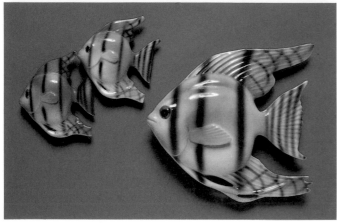

Everything (or almost everything) in pairs—it seems that people like order, but do not like simple, boring geometry; they prefer asymmetrical motifs made symmetrical by being part of a pair (or, sometimes, a triad). Basically, this was usually Noah's Ark stuff: boy meets girl, and they pair off. In some cases the manufacturer did the minimum necessary to turn a male form into a female form (or vice versa) in order to offer a set. The results—seen on the facing page—could be rather odd: androgynous, indeed.

President Eisenhower was the right
leader for the times—an era
adventurous in terms of business and
manufacturing expansion, but
essentially conservative in tenor. The
home, though elaborated with
lighthearted ornament, was not a place
to be mocked.

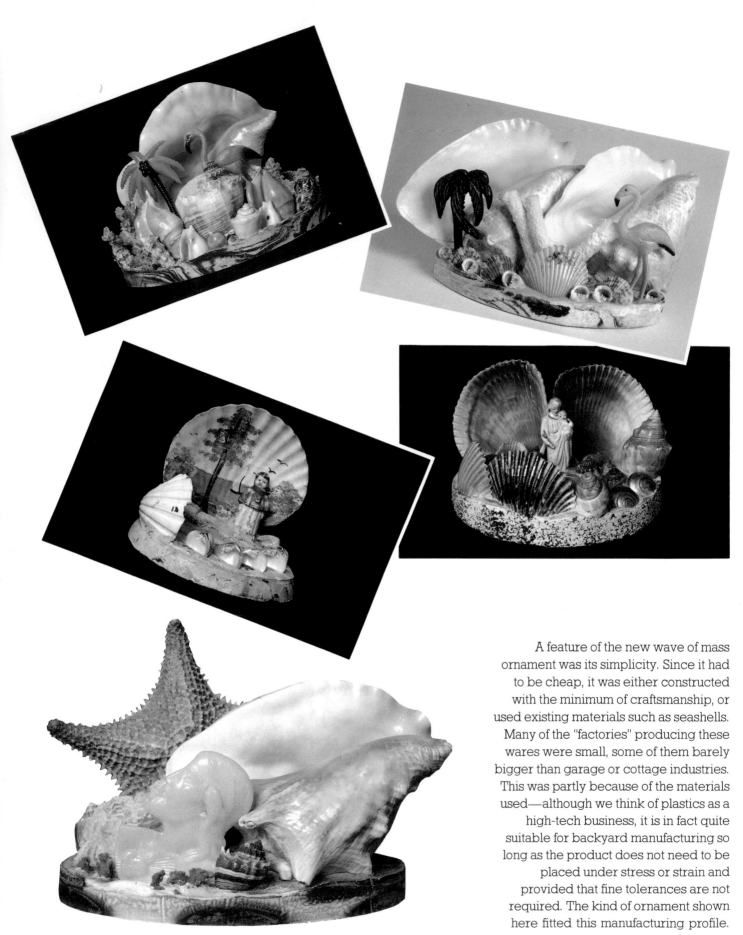

A feature of the new wave of mass ornament was its simplicity. Since it had to be cheap, it was either constructed with the minimum of craftsmanship, or used existing materials such as seashells. Many of the "factories" producing these wares were small, some of them barely bigger than garage or cottage industries. This was partly because of the materials used—although we think of plastics as a high-tech business, it is in fact quite suitable for backyard manufacturing so long as the product does not need to be placed under stress or strain and provided that fine tolerances are not required. The kind of ornament shown here fitted this manufacturing profile.

The flickering "Forest Fire" lamp was a popular novelty. The electric light bulb gets hot; the hot air moves; the moving air catches the lightweight "turbine" above it and appears to make the light flicker; and the flicker, seen through the plastic shade, looks like fire.

Depiction of other races—generally with contented, nubile or exotic, but not threatening, overtones—was a common feature of the ornament.

These are details from Hawaiian shirts: loud, happy and exuberant. Neutral subjects, such as plants, landscapes and fruit, are obvious candidates for mass-manufactured decoration because they are least likely to offend, and most likely to sell.

In the Fifties the micro chip was not even a glimmer in a Sci-Fi writer's eye; even the new transistors were, by comparison, suitcase-size. Mechanical things still had big motors, and clocks, like anything else with moving parts, were bulky. You could, however, disguise them as miniature TVs—and some good straightforward functional designs were in evidence, too. Patriotism continued to be important in the life of the nation: the child's bedside lamp opposite was a constant reminder of allegiance.

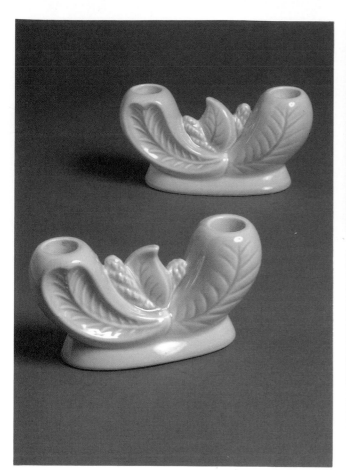

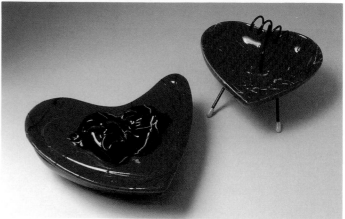

Manufacturers got clever at
niche marketing—spotting
gaps in the market created by
other new products and trends. The
TV was very useful in this regard: the
TV dinner cup 'n' platter set (*above*)
would sit easily on the rampant arm of the
monster TV lounge armchair. In similar fashion,
the telephone generated a host of telephone
extras, like this "Miss Kitty" ballpoint pen and letter
holder. Effective use was made of complementary
colours—yellow, magenta and black.

Attenuated form was a stylistic feature of much Fifties design. But since abstraction was not an easy style to sell, the long thin forms favored by the modernists, the high priests of design, found their expression in more familiar and obviously recognizable motifs. Hence Flamingos—elongated and pink. These birds also provided a taste of foreign lands. It hardly mattered whether you went abroad; manufacturing industry offered you a galaxy of souvenirs on Main Street.

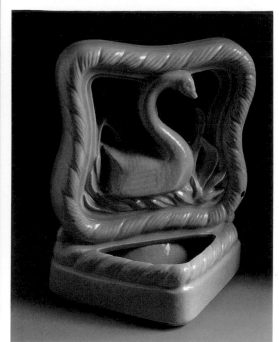

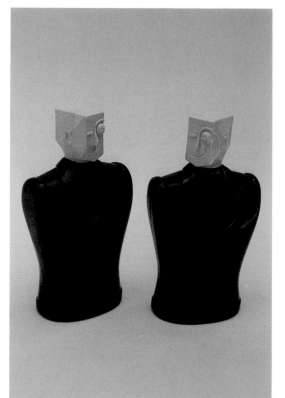

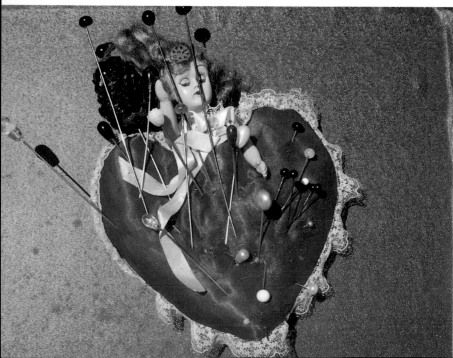

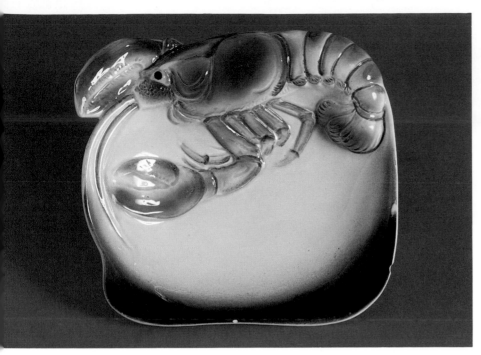

By no means all the ornament that poured out of the factories was bland. In a proportion of the objects, especially the religious ones, there are hints of something darker. Christianity and Voodoo melt down to produce a decidedly edgy confection in some of the Hawaiian ornament. The heart-shaped pincushion (*opposite, bottom*) is not so much domestically comforting as worrying for its suggestion of witchcraft.

Hollywood, of course, had learned quickly that we really love to frighten the wits out of ourselves. The Halloween lamp (*above right*) and plastic skeleton (*opposite, above left*) bric-a-brac are part of the house-of-horror fall out.

The blockheaded scent bottles (*opposite, center right*) are uncomfortable, not for any hint of voodoo, but because they are robot-like. As the decade went on, models of the human form became less and less literal as the public grew accustomed to ever-increasing levels of abstraction in day-to-day imagery, especially in TV advertising and cartoons.

53

The dining room is yet another room which, in our current house, in most American middle-majority homes, and most certainly in the homes of the Fifties, is under-used. The real hub is the kitchen, or wherever the TV lands up. But high days and holidays are feasted in the dining room: as in the world over, the best linen and china, the most elaborate ornament, is set out for the fancy of the guests.

But, whenever one regards the Fifties in America, one is looking at style which is proselytized by the TV, but actually centers on the American automobile. The automobile was defined by its chrome—lots of swollen, fantastic and streamlined chrome. Much has been written about the era of the all-American car, epitomized by the designs of Harley Earl (Vice President Styling of General Motors). The Fifties was the decade in which the great interstate freeways were built. Speed, or the appearance of speed, infected America and found its way—swiftly—into the home, especially into the kitchen.

The gas cooker, for example, is a bulbous, streamlined hulk with the general characteristics of an Oldsmobile. "For cooking delight," went the 1952 ad., "I'll take Tappan. Only Tappan has Chrome OVEN interior." And the plush plastic chromium-bound dining chairs that look like tightly corseted frankfurters take their cue from the car seat and the interstate diner. This was the future: real speedy. Even many of the jugs and coffee flasks lean forward at an angle, peering into the future, pushing away from the past, their very moldings reminiscent of automobile body work.

One of the characteristics of American design which has made a substantial return in the late 1980s and which has never left fringe design (the crafts, for example) is the predominance of shapes that look as though they are to be put into the mouth and sucked. Even automobiles look as if they were made to be sucked, like ice lollies.

NEW HORNET SPECIAL
available in Four-Door Sedan, Club Sedan and Club Coupe—all at new low prices

"FOR COOKING DELIGHT...
I'll take TAPPAN"

GAS RANGE
Your guide to the best in modern automatic cookery

Oral gratification seemed to be the
general theme of many of these salvaged
treasures of advertising from the Fifties, now
crowded into our dining room. Whether it be Coca Cola
("for the pause that refreshes"), or Camel cigarettes, there was a dominant "suck
it and see," come-on-in advertising. Smoking was socially acceptable, it was
glamorous, it was an orally sensate glamor often promoted by celebrities from
the movies. If the dream is creamy in several of its parts, the Fifties contribution
looks like a celebration of a great American breast.

The development and consumption of fast food was encouraged by the
fashion for speed and also for novelty. To be new was a great selling point, and to
be instant was very heaven. Moreover, food was no longer permitted to interrupt
daily life. Mom did not want to spend long hours in the kitchen preparing food
and missing TV; and the kids, whether they were into the local TV station's rock
'n' roll sessions or into bowling, wanted to eat on the run.

Fast food and snacks and TV meals were also encouraged by rapid
improvements in color photography—magazines like *Women's Day*, *Ladies
Home Journal* and *Today's Woman* were filled with the visual promises of
elaborate cakes and delicacies that looked like the crafted confections of master
chefs but were available in packets such as Duff's Devils Food Mix or Swans
Down Fluff O Mint Cake. In fact food technology was *not* all that advanced—
when you read the small print there was still some cooking to do. There was also
a lot of concern about economical eating; families were not awash with bucks,
most of which were committed to the repayments.

Color added to the general agitation: cars were colored, food was colored, the utensils and the crockery were colored. Everything was zippy. The Eisenhower years were a kind of childhood for all Americans. To that extent, looking around the Fifties kitchen, we have more than a passing sense of something toylike, childlike—a kind of grown-up nursery.

This sense is also present in the details of the kitchen, like the wives' aprons. Naturally there are two kinds of apron—the kitchen pinny and the formal one for wearing in the dining room for guests. These pinafores are frequently flirtatious; we have one example—the panty apron—which is some way from the sobriety of Mom and apple pie.

The adults of the 1950s, our Ma's and Pa's, Moms and Dads, our blessed parents, may have been childlike in their acceptance of the new (certainly advertising presumed them to be so), but what, of course, marks out the man (or the woman) from the child is sex. Running through the decoration and playful ornament, there is often a heavy touch of sex, though it is always presented from the man's point of view. Thus we have a nudie salt 'n' pepper set, and glass tumblers decorated with women who, viewed from one side, mysteriously lose their clothes.

What is interesting also is that in middle-majority America these jokey objects oscillated between the kitchen and the dining room. The dining room may have been more formally laid out for a meal, but it was not pompous; this America is, we presume, more relaxed than its European counterpart.

Again, our own kitchen and dining room are excessive, and the dining room has occasional touches that are not to do with the Fifties we have been describing—such as the artist's palette chair and the Peacock wicker seat. Moreover, the richly made-up faces of celebrities fill our walls. We have brought the advertisement off the streets and into our home, thus bringing fantasy and reality face to face.

It's something of a stage set, of course. Something for people to talk about, as you would expect: for this is the dining room, and what makes a meal memorable as much as culinary sophistication is the good conversation—even if it's dirty chuckles over the shakers.

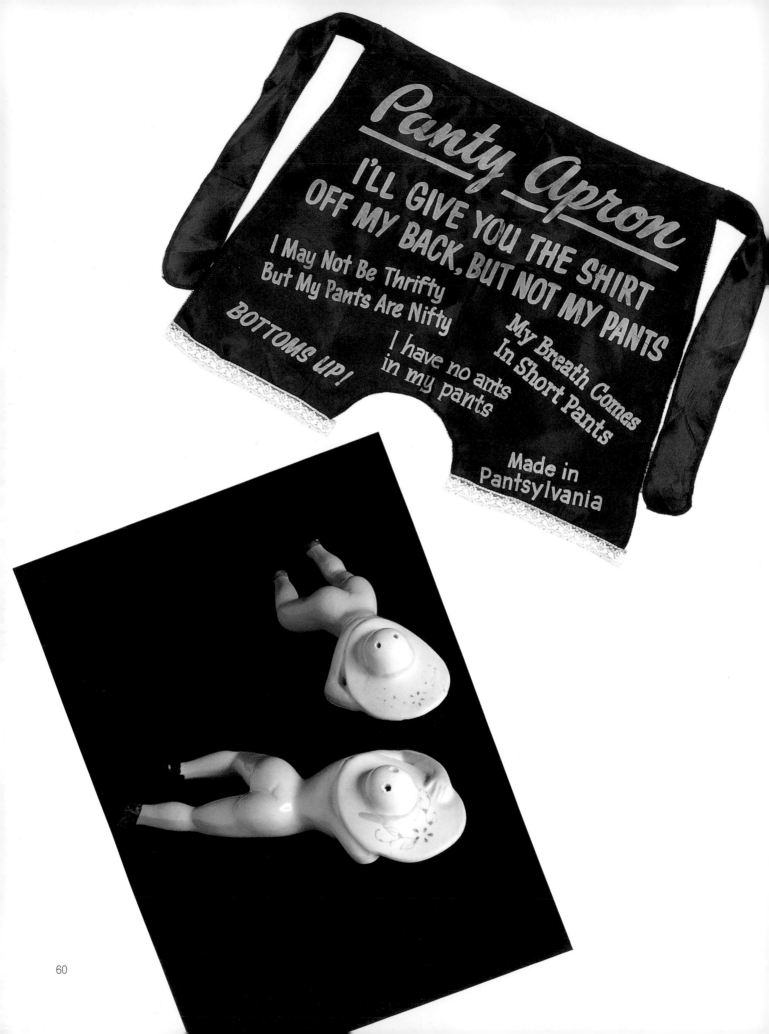

Like it Lively?

The consistent feature of the consumer boom in the Fifties was the certainty that someone, somewhere would always turn over a dollar by making a novelty out of the most mundane of everyday objects. Plastic gradually replaced plaster and ceramic as the obvious cheap material for these novelties.

The nudie salt 'n' pepper sets (*opposite, bottom*) confirm that a lot of the humor was at the expense of women. Much of the lighthearted ornament is defined by innuendo that appeals first and mainly to men. Women had three roles in the home—cook, mother, and sexual companion. These three strings became the manufacturer's master chord in playing the domestic market. Sex, however, was only hinted at, and remained flirty in the Fifties.

The chrome and plush plastic of the American car, the dirigible of the freeway, influenced a lot of design in the home, especially in the kitchen. The kitchen was the first room in the house to be open to new materials, and to design that was clearly machine-like and modern in its imagery. High tech became acceptable in the kitchen, but remained unacceptable in the lounge.

The automobile presented a potent image because the auto was synonymous with NEWNESS. Car makers had learned to style up a new model every year in order to keep feeding the desire for the NEW, and the same passion for novelty was encouraged in all aspects of consumer spending.

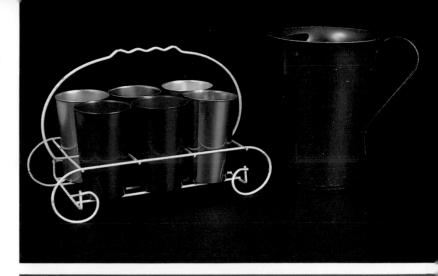

In the late Eighties there is a new generation of architects and designers producing contemporary designs which, in fact, replicate many of the shapes and forms typified by such Fifties artefacts as these flasks (*below*).

Elsewhere, in the ever-expanding children's market, the manufacturers were quick to celebrate technological successes. The military, with their new nuclear-powered submarines, developed a passion for record-breaking journeys under the polar ice. Hence the subs on the metal lunchbox (*opposite, bottom*).

USS GEORGE WASHINGTON

DuPont was then, and is today, a world leader in the development of new and advanced materials. It was also one of the companies that learned early on to speak directly to the general public, even if the users of its products were other manufacturers. This strategy, of course, eased the acceptance of new materials and made manufacturers keen to use new products such as Cellophane.

Little girls, sugar and spice, and all of that, made good advertising copy. Little girls were eased into becoming little wives by their toys, such as the toy tin cooker (*opposite*).

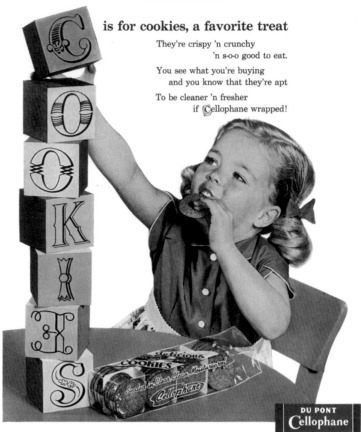

is for cookies, a favorite treat

They're crispy 'n crunchy
    'n s-o-o good to eat.

You see what you're buying
    and you know that they're apt

To be cleaner 'n fresher
    if Cellophane wrapped!

DU PONT
Cellophane

The eyes certainly have it. Everywhere we looked, the world was presented as friendly or cute.

Although most of the elaboration and decoration was not very realistic, there was also a demand for surfaces which simulated other surfaces. The replacement of real wicker work with plastic wicker (*above*) is one example, but there were also the visual puns—turning a lunchbox into a sliced loaf (*opposite, bottom*).

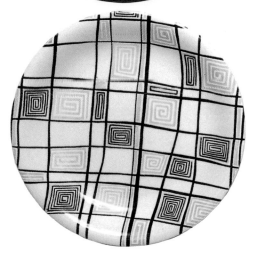

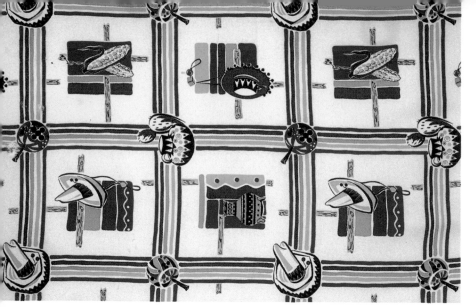

Aprons and tablecloths, cheap, cheerful and wholesome. There are hidden influences from the new technology buried in the design of these humble wares. The Fifties went for washing machines and detergents in a big way—it saved labor—but the materials best suited for washing machines were color-fast and uncomplicated. When you designed an apron, you thought first— can this be machine-washed? The modern age may have more decorated surfaces, but it has fewer genuine complications of form— the washer will not take them.

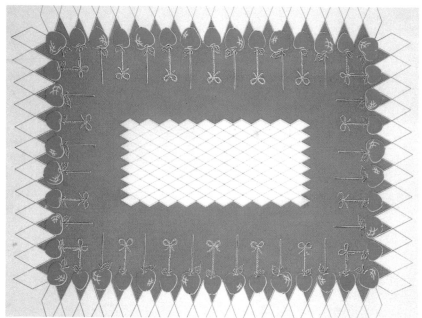

Color was everything. It was one of the chemical industry's gifts to us, clear deep reds and yellows and greens. Quite often the color was put to good effect in simple designs—the cups and saucers opposite are now regarded, rightly, as little design classics: practical, pretty and cheap.

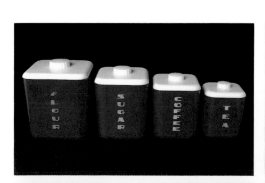

However zany the product, there is usually a logic of sorts at work. But once in a while in our collecting we come across objects whose rationale at first makes us pause. Why have a clock, we ask, masquerading as a teapot—except, of course, as a good old one-liner: TEA TIME. The creamer (*opposite, center left*) is a tougher one to crack. We have thought of Humpty Dumpty, but he was an egg, and the connection between eggs and milk, if close, is not that close. The other visual references are easy to grasp— the polar bears (*center left*) go nicely with the ice cubes, and the pink elephants (*above left*) are an alcoholic tease. The Dutch, a nation whose culture is synonymous with good housekeeping, dance on the plastic "Delft" ware (*opposite, bottom*).

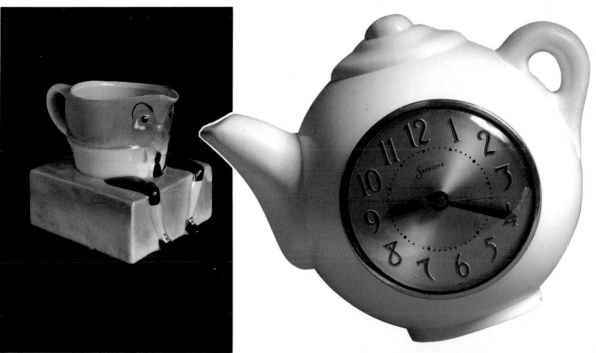

No matter who decorated the rest of the house or in what fashion, the "master" (but not master's) bedroom was and is an area where a person's individual personality is paramount. Indeed, it is the one place where one can let go. The sluttish can relax from the rigor of trying to create order, whilst the orderly, fed up with the unthinking anarchy of the rest of the family, can reign in disciplined tidiness.

Middle-majority America sleeps in pairs; it may favor separate beds, but not separate bedrooms. Even so, the bedroom is predominantly regarded as a feminine room; it's been molded by Hollywood and TV, and these media have set the standards for exotic glamor. It is the heart of the American dream, where the twin roles of the princess and the harlot (scripted by men, aided by romantic novelists) entwine. Mother meets wife. Next to Godliness, cleanliness vies with lubricious coyness. This American bedroom is an ambiguous territory; it might look innocent but innocence is not what it's about.

The Hollywood mystique of the *femme fatale*, the blonde bombshell with the painted nails, the fingers languorous upon the white sheet, or the silken leg draped across the tiger-stripe fun fur, is a manmade image. The subdued indirect lighting provided by the bamboo-based floor lamp provides the atmosphere for any romantic intent. Left to their own devices for image making, women would probably not have caricatured seduction quite so crudely.

Yet it was accepted or at any rate not questioned that the bedroom was the venue for a sense of the exotic. The things in it generally gesture towards luxury: the buttoned-down white padded vinyl headboards (should have been leather), the brushed nylon leopard-skin bedcovers are two examples. There are also the dressing tables—these always look impracticable because they are deeply scalloped to draw the sitter into the mirror and have insufficient tabletop space to put cosmetics. Each dressing table is a confection of curves on insubstantial legs that make the place look as though it is simpering on high heels.

Fifties women's magazines, in articles on interior decor, stressed the importance of having an attractive bedroom—always reminding readers that they spent a third of their lives there. Through the fashion pages the American lady was encouraged to view the place as a boudoir in which she might flit in elaborate nightgown and wraps. For our collection we have acquired a surprising array of the night and bedroom attire: not kinky, but romantic, suggesting a vast regiment of amateur unknown domestic actresses (and some actors).

The bedroom was also a place for keeping God. There is a great variety of plastic religious ornament for the home, especially the Catholic home. The further away from Europe one gets, the more vivid or hybrid the religious ornament becomes. Near Mexico the plastic crucifixions come in a variety of meaty bloodiness, whilst from Hawaii we see Catholic Christianity sieved through a mesh of Haitian voodoo, resulting in bizarre domestic shrines-cum-lamps. Other domestic shrines are less mortal in their emphasis and often double as lamps—the Virgin Mary or a figure of Christ backlit in a sea of seashells is a common example.

Piety and the bedroom come together. It is obviously the most intimate room, one where the souvenirs, the gilded frames of the photographs of dead relatives and the sentimental ornaments of courtship have a poignancy that defies the design aficionado to write them off as merely trashy.

But, naturally, the bedroom was also the focus of manufacturers ever anxious to sell the housewife labor-saving devices. Lady Pepperell FORM FIT sheets were the answer to the question: WANT TO SAVE YOUR-SELF WORK? No daily tucking (they were fitted), no ironing (they were Sanforized). Women were encouraged to buy gadgets to make themselves more beautiful; some bought enough to set up a hairdressing salon.

The Fifties also saw a big increase in the agitation over how we smelt. Tussy instantly stops perspiration odor! Keep your <u>Whole</u> mouth <u>wholesome!</u> with the double protection of Ipana. How a wife can hold on to married happiness—use Zonite for a cleansing, antiseptic and deodorizing douche! The exclamation mark punctuated daily life.

Listerine advertisements must have screwed up many a person's day with their strident, interrogative copy: "How's your breath today? Never take it for granted. Never risk offending others, needlessly. Halitosis is the fault unpardonable." Bad breath lost you dates and jobs, and ruined marriages. Halitosis was much worse than the Atom bomb.

And so, into our bathrooms we fled. To utilize the miracles of modern science and make ourselves "nice to be near." What better place to perform these daily acts of contrition that make one "socially acceptable" than these palaces of gleaming chrome and glossy two-tone pastel tilework? Palaces, indeed! To the extent that in many homes the bathroom became known as the "throne room," thereby cementing the concept of the porcelain keep, and creating a "cute" euphemism for the toilet, so typical of the period. No Bodily Functions, please.

The huge choice of material and colors available to the homeowner was certainly apparent in bathroom fixtures and appointments. We favored light, cheerful color-schemes: pink-and-blue (milady's favorite, and extensible to the nursery), yellow-and-gray, mint green-and-white, or pink-and-black for that sense of high drama while you shower. Chrome fittings reflected light off a thousand sparkling edges. Double lamps flanking the mirror made make-up application a breeze, and shaving a joy. The only thing that might possibly obscure the vision of a sparkling-clean "You" was decorator mirror decals, featuring standard motifs of an aquatic nature—bubbles, fish, swans, and coy mermaids. If not water-related, these darling decals might feature a French Poodle (Oh-la-la!) daintily applying cosmetic touches to her muzzle before a mirror not unlike your own! Art imitates Life, after all. These same motifs were not regulated strictly to the mirror, either. Your walls, covered in lovely faux marble Formica, could rival Davy Jones' locker, swimming with exotic fish groups (always one large, and two small), or mermaid families cavorting with pearls 'n' bubbles. Your Nu-Tru plastic shower curtain was awash with sea horses, raindrops, or graceful swans, skillfully shielding modest You from prying eyes.

Nature abhors a vacuum, and so did Mrs Fifties Housewife, filling these sanitary sanctuaries with brightly colored towels, bric-a-brac, plastic pearlized lotion-and-cotton dispensers, crocheted dolls-of-all-Nations toilet tissue covers, and everything imaginable to entertain the senses during those extended visits to a private function.

When we finally emerged, it was not unlike the end of a small vacation. Or leaving the hospital, whose sterilized corridors could scarcely be cleaner than our Grottoes for Keeping Clean.

Now that we had become all things physically desirable, it was time to return to our bedrooms. Once more within the privacy of our respective fantasies, we could prepare to lay out and don fabulous garments, stylish and sporty, capable of telling the world who-we-were. The sense of novelty, design, and color already seen in home decoration had crossed over into fashion and personal adornment, as well.

Adults, Moms and Dads, could attire themselves in the newest "casual" sportswear; the influx of longer periods of free time, and utilization of time-saving household devices created a market for specialized clothing, reflecting the new lifestyle of personal freedom, and the devil-may-care attitude that accompanied it. For Dad, the day's choice might be an iridescent red lounge-lizard jacket, with blue argyle shirt and patterned tie. Dressy, but relaxed. Mother could find her finishing touches, the lovely "Parisian" patterned vinyl handbag and good white gloves waiting on the dresser. Smart, snappy, and ready to go!

Meanwhile, the kids were busy dividing themselves into the two warring factions of the period, either clean-cut citizens of tomorrow or juvenile delinquents. For those goody-two-shoe boys, we had patterned two-tone gabardine jackets, often reversible. Underneath, how about a really keen red Lurex spangle shirt (which was composed of a metal and natural thread combination, first seen covering chairs and couches more suitable for a rocketship than the living room. Could this be Body Upholstery?); and to top it off, a lively bow tie. Miss Prim 'n' Proper teen queen might don her best pastel dish hat and smart plastic rhinestone bag for the afternoon outing. Very pert! On the other side of the tracks, for those "Ladies" of a more lawless disposition, we have a jungle of assorted leopard-skin prints, "naughty" undies, and prerequisite killer high heels. Just what no "nice" girl would think of wearing. For Bad Boys, sleazy rayon sports shirts of abstract print, and the Black Leather Jacket, a classic form of fashion rebellion from its very inception.

Although the choice of accessories, jewelry, watches, lighters, cigarette cases, etc., remained personal touches not everyone felt necessary, there was one iconographic element agreed on by all. Sunglasses, for the masses. No outfit was complete without them, and they came in a blinding and bewildering assortment of styles and statements. Americans took sunglasses seriously, as visible evidence of leisure time in abundance, and the RIGHT element to supply a sense of glamor and mystery to anyone. We were all Hollywood stars, and in most cases, for less than a dollar.

The Fifties offered to all, the modern solution to telling society Who one Really Was, by virtue of the shirt on one's back. New materials, easy-to-care-for fabrics, and the ever-increasing allowance of free time coupled with more money and more places to spend it, made dressing right more important than ever, but compensated for by being so E-Z! Even though the Fifties home was certainly an oasis of luxury living in a troubled world, with clothes like these it's a wonder anyone stayed home at all.

Many things were approached flirtatiously rather than directly; designs for the bathroom and bedroom were often visual euphemisms.

Love was a euphemism, too—the ideal, caught in this Hollywood motif (*above*), was dream-like pleasure. We were so innocent still; none of us, not even the adults, especially the adults, wanted to grow up.

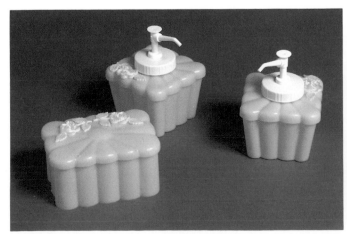

Plastic Angel Gabriels watched over us at night whilst doubling as light switches (*right*). Meanwhile, our cowboy clock (*below left*) whirled its electrically powered lasso round and round and round. Everything had to move—if not, it had at least to appear to move. Cartoon animation had a lot of influence. Children, though naturally full of energy, got used to things on TV happening fast: life was shown as being one event after another. We were not prepared for the blank bits that real life offered; boredom had apparently been banished.

And we loved the glitziness of it all. Our big sisters and their boyfriends came on loud and strong, especially on the beach or in the summer streets on vacation—America invented wild sunglass frames, and excess reigned.

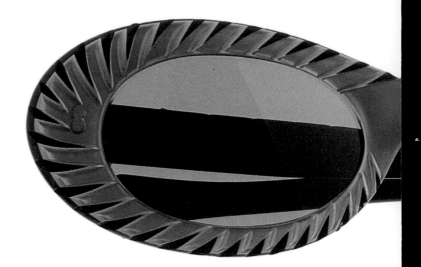

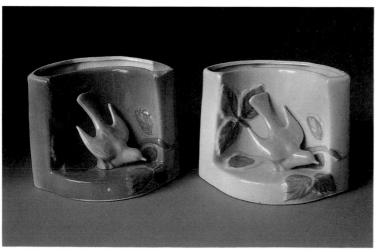

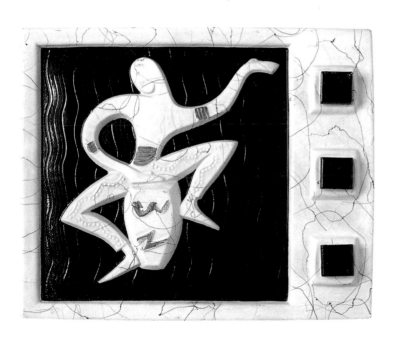

When Fifties America dressed up, it had style. We see these collections as falling into the bad boy/good boy and bad girl/good girl categories. The young, the American teenager, grabbed fashion, and the clothing industry loved them for it. Young America had discovered posing, swinging, the hip look, the soft shuffle and the cool amble along the sidewalk. The boys had greater freedom and were uniformly casual, but good girls still kept a formality about themselves when dressed up. For most people, denim came later.

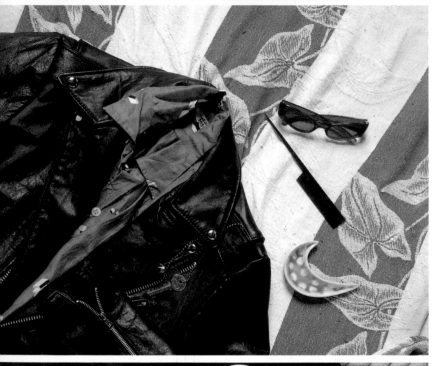

Collector's Guide

All collecting is to some extent a personal matter—the more so in the fast-developing field of Fifties objects and memorabilia. To begin with, our own approach – and how this worked out in practice—may offer some guidance to the neophyte.

There is no particular rhyme or reason to the objects we fixate upon, or collect. The chance discovery of an unknown and thrilling "thing" can spark pursuit of similar "things" with a vengeance. Said pursuit will continue until a newer and better "thing" comes along. We have found that in building such a collection, it's best to make no demands, for in a country bountiful with oddity, there is no shortage of "things"! Like iron to a magnet, so do objects come to us.

However, if these pieces of history fail to show up on the doorstep, or clutched in the arms of well-meaning friends ("I found something really awful and thought of you"), we comb the countryside, believing that one person's trash is another's treasure. Truly. We have dared to go where no one in their right minds would venture, prying into dark, ugly boxes and under tables on the verge of collapse. Some objects must be coaxed out of thrift shops, or from the recesses of neighborhood garage sales. We delight in large, sprawling curbside junk-piles, and have learned to spot valuable furniture and lampshades while speeding by in the family truck. Leave no stone unturned. Never pass up the opportunity to look in on any flea market or junket sale, for the day you do, you will miss that mate to that Spanish dancer lamp, and your life will be poorer for having missed it.

This collection was built, piece by piece, in just this fashion. To understand fully the illogicalness, humor, anxiety, and sense of high drama of the much-maligned Fifties style, we feel that there is no other way to obtain objects. Whenever possible, we try to retrieve pieces from the original owners, who usually have pointed reasons for letting these treasures slip away ("... it just looks so old-fashioned! How could we have ever spent good money on that?").

As the public's esthetic taste is changed and shaped by industry, the ever-pressing need to "modernize" continues, even in low-income households. There's no use in wondering why people could possibly let go of these wonderful objects, for we realize that the heart of home decorating is in a state of constant flux. The American public, trained for so long to keep up with the neighbors, will keep absorbing the "new" and rejecting the "old" in a vain attempt to stay "current." There is truly a story behind everything here in our collection.

Unfortunately, the very reason that made so much available to so many during the Fifties, makes some objects virtually unobtainable today. Cheap materials and a burgeoning sense of planned obsolescence inherent in the objects themselves, make many decorative and household artefacts rare. Since they were never meant to last, their existence today has rendered some survivors valuable.

Even though the Fifties are not so very far away in time, many historians and designers have chosen to belittle the style, or worse, ignore it completely. It seems to be common thought from esteemed quarters that such a frivolous period cannot yield anything of value from a "serious" design standpoint, especially since not enough years have passed to give an unbiased view overall. However, as time advances, and post-modernism continues to "borrow" from this wealth of visual information, interest in the period and its treasures is always increasing. What were once cast-offs gathering dust in second-hand shops are now gathering big money in glittering antique emporiums, many specializing solely in the period. As the buying public is again re-educated to the novelty of design and emotion from its own self-forgotten past, the availability of the Real Stuff will decrease.

For those individuals who are curious, interested, or have been converted by this book, we offer the following guidelines for obtaining a piece of the period.

Try to familiarize yourself with the style. Fifties artefacts are usually easy to spot, by color (bright and unnatural) and by shape (soft, "free-form," and "outer-spacey.") Look for florid patterns of unknown plant life, animal-skin, or anything that resembles "modern art." Read. Your local library can supply you with many pictorial volumes of design, architecture, and material usage of the period. Or, try re-reading this book! Learn what to look for, and you won't go home empty-handed.

The easiest places to find Fifties treasure is in the specialty antique shop or boutique that deals solely in that period. There is really no use in listing names of shops currently dealing these objects, since the details are fast-changing. Often the market demand for particular things dries up, forcing shop owners to close. At the time of writing this, however, the renewed interest in the Fifties has helped put many such shops in business, often bearing names that refer to the period itself, including "Boomerang," "Moderne," "Retro," and "Cowboys and Poodles."

These stores usually charge high prices. You will be paying for the object, its condition, its clean-up, and possibly its restoration (look carefully!), and naturally you are paying for the effort the dealer had to put in to obtain the thing. Many people prefer to obtain objects this way, since they haven't the time—or inclination—to do research in rougher places, and they also like choosing from a lot of desirable objects gathered together in one place. Often these objects are of good quality, sometimes rare, and require no effort other than making up one's mind, paying and taking the selection home to be admired.

In most countries, major cities have districts in which the antique trade is centered, and it is within these centers that you may find specialty shops. The following are examples within the US:
NEW YORK CITY: Greenwich Village and the Canal Street district.
PHILADELPHIA: Society Hill's Pine Street and South Street areas.
CHICAGO: Halstead Street and Oldtown areas.

SAN FRANCISCO: Market Street, Castro Street, and Haight Street areas.
LOS ANGELES: Hollywood and Melrose Street areas.
If visiting, check the local phone book for listings, or enquire at a visitor center.

Thrift shops and flea markets are venues for the adventurous collector who is not afraid of hard work, tired feet, and frequent frustration. These inconveniences are compensated for by the wonderful things at reasonable (or very low) prices. Your local phone book can offer addresses for thrift or secondhand shops that deal in objects or furniture, as well as clothing. Large "recognized" thrift shops may be found in most cities, large and small, and change their stock at an astonishing pace. American examples include: Goodwill, Salvation Army, and St. Vincent DePaul.

Flea markets have become larger in recent years; they offer trash and treasure intermixed, sometimes accompanied by crafts, food, and entertainment. One might spend long hours at the largest such affairs, haggling over prices (a time-honored tradition) and uncovering artefacts. Most flea markets are local attractions, and the well-known ones draw dealers and buyers from great distances. Most take place outside during the warmer months, on a regular once-a-week or once-a-month basis. Examples include: The Washington Courthouse Market in Ohio; The Kane County Flea Market in Illinois; Portobello Road in London; and certainly the great Flea Market of Paris. There are far too many such markets to list here, but the classified ads in your local newspaper should list the ones in your area. Check under "Antiques and Collectibles," and especially at weekends. Or, look for antique magazine listings at your local newsstand or bookstore.

Last, but not least, look at garage sales, junket sales, white elephant sales or whatever such sales are called where you live. These curious opportunities pop up in unexpected places at odd times, and usually in local neighborhoods, or run by organizations such as schools or churches. There are no schedules, so you must be aware of activities occurring in your area. They are good places to find terrific objects, "still warm" from the original owners. This is great for collectors, for often one may find out the history (or provenance) for the mere price of the object. Prices themselves tend to be very, very low, and often selection is plentiful. Check local bulletin boards in shops or the classified ads in your newspaper.

A Final Piece of Advice From Two Who Know: "When you see it, buy it, because it won't be there when you go back."

Good Luck, and remember to leave something for us!

List of Illustrations

Advertisements or illustrations on pp.4, 10, 59, 82 from *Ladies' Home Journal*, July 1950; on pp.5, 9, 31, 32, 33 (*center*), 81 (*top right*) from *Small Homes Guide*, Winter 1950–Spring 1951; on pp.11, 57, 58, 80, 81 (*bottom left*) from *Woman's Day*, March 1952; on pp.30, 33 (*top left, bottom right*) from *Today's Woman*, April 1953; and on pp.33 (*top right*), 56 from *The Saturday Evening Post*, August 28, 1954.

Color photographs by Norinne Betjemann, except for the above; p.63, *bottom left* (Thomas Brummett); pp.26, *right*; 37, *bottom*; 47, *bottom*; 50, *left*; 52, *bottom left*; 53, *top right, bottom*; 68, *bottom right* (Mark Burns).